DIGITAL NOMADS

DIGITAL NOMADS

Mastering the Art of Working from Anywhere

B. VINCENT

QuantumQuill Press

CONTENTS

1   Introduction   1

2   Benefits of Being a Digital Nomad   3

3   Essential Skills for Digital Nomads   5

4   Finding Remote Work Opportunities   6

5   Setting Up a Productive Remote Workspace   8

6   Managing Time and Productivity as a Digital Nomad   10

7   Balancing Work and Personal Life   12

8   Overcoming Challenges of Working from Anywhere   14

9   Maintaining a Healthy Lifestyle as a Digital Nomad   16

10   Building a Network and Community   18

11   Financial Considerations for Digital Nomads   20

12   Legal and Visa Requirements for Digital Nomads   22

13   Travel Tips and Destinations for Digital Nomads   24

14   Digital Nomad Tools and Resources   26

15   Success Stories and Inspirations   28

16   Conclusion   30

CHAPTER 1

Introduction

Digital Nomads: Mastering the art of working from anywhere is written in such a way that it is both a guide to the digital nomad lifestyle and to the digital nomad himself. The author, Mish Slade, has utilized her many years of experience in numerous different forms of nomadic working to provide an in-depth analysis of what it means to be a digital nomad. Mish refers to 'the art of working from anywhere', giving the reader an idea that to be a successful digital nomad, it requires a certain level of skill and dedication. Building the foundations of the book around the reader, she is able to relate to the experiences told to her by over 50 other digital nomads who provided their stories to be shared in the book. These "bolt hole" stories, as they are referred to, give an indication of both success and failure in the lifestyle. This, in turn, allows for a solid platform of advice to be shared with the reader.

Digital Nomads: Mastering the art of working from anywhere provides an insight into the world of those who are not bound by offices or desk jobs. This book is a guide to the digital nomad life-style. For those of you who don't know, a digital nomad is a person who is free from the usual constraints of working in an office 9-5, for a single employer in a single location. They use telecommunications technology to earn a living. This is a lifestyle which appeals to many but it is not as easy as it first appears. This book illustrates the pros and cons of this lifestyle. It is a guide for those who have only just embarked on this way of living and a reference for those who are already on their way.

CHAPTER 2

Benefits of Being a Digital Nomad

Most people in their lifetime have toyed with the idea of escaping the rat race, packing it in, causing a shift in their life's direction, venturing out, seeing what lies beyond the horizon... It is the free-spirited and adventurous. But due to societal pressures, familial responsibilities, and career progress, it often proves to be too great a risk. It's a common feeling to reflect and wonder what life might have been had we acquired the courage to make bold choices and follow our instincts in each given moment. The digital nomad leaves one life behind to start another and live to tell the tale. This can shape into an aspiration to be a pioneer of sorts and leave a trail for others to follow, and a nomadic lifestyle professional is no exception.

A common reason the digital nomad lifestyle has become so appealing is the ability to escape the corporate grind. This type of career often goes hand-in-hand with the 9-5 workday and long hours at the office. Many office workers find themselves becoming jaded and fed up with the constraints of working for someone else, and the monotony of paying bills and saving for trips around the much coveted 2-3 weeks of vacation time per year.

The flexibility to do what you want, when you want, and to live where you please - this sums up the freedom intrinsic to the digital nomad lifestyle. There are numerous benefits to becoming a digital nomad and making a living on the road. The following list will give you an idea of the many positive aspects of pursuing this path.

CHAPTER 3

Essential Skills for Digital Nomads

Not just anyone can pick up and travel the world while working remotely. Not all work schedules and personalities are conducive to traveling and living the so-called "Digital Nomad" lifestyle. There are certain skills and mindsets that lend themselves to the freedom and flexibility of working from anywhere. In this chapter, I'll share some of the most important qualities to have developed, or be willing to develop, while seeking a life of freedom. With these changes in priorities and focus, you can maximize your potential for success and adventure, and minimize the difficulty of leaving the comfort and structures of the office environment. Digital nomads tend to learn these lessons through necessity, myself included, but you can set yourself up for an easy transition by considering and working on these things now.

CHAPTER 4

Finding Remote Work Opportunities

Another strategy is to leverage your current skills and experience into a more suitable telecommuting or contract job. Networking with people in your current or desired industry is key. Your chances of success will be much higher if you have proven yourself in the industry and have developed strong working relationships. Job search websites are an obvious starting point, and there are a few that specialize in remote work. Be aware, however, that many of these sites are plagued by virtual "assembly lines" of workers competing for salary-jeopardizing levels. And since the jobs are often outsourced from western countries, they do not tend to last long as the cost of living increases in the worker's home country.

One strategy is to negotiate a remote work arrangement with your current employer. Emphasize the cost-saving benefits, improved efficiency, and your own track record of productivity as a bargaining chip. Just remember, effective telecommuting requires a high level of autonomy and confidence in your work, strong communication skills, and equal or greater results than if you were in the office.

Apply these principles to your current job to demonstrate that you can make it work.

Don't despair if you're in the middle of your career and have just had an epiphany that you want to be location-independent. The bad news is that it may be difficult to convert your present job into a telecommuting position. This is because employers trying out the remote arrangement usually prefer to test it out on workers who are new to the company and who don't require as much hand-holding. The good news, however, is that there are remote jobs to be found if you are determined and resourceful.

CHAPTER 5

Setting Up a Productive Remote Workspace

If you have the option to create a dedicated office in your location, it will make things much simpler for you. When you work in a shared space with a roommate or family, it can reduce your productivity when not everyone's schedule aligns. It can be difficult to get quiet time, and without a lock on the door, it's common to be interrupted mid-task. An office with a door is always the best for deep concentration work. A lock on the door may not be necessary, but it's important to establish with others in your living space when you are not to be disturbed. A spare bedroom can make a great office, but if you don't have this type of luxury, even a corner of a room can be a great workspace with the right setup. The living room and high traffic areas are not ideal for focused work, so try to avoid these spots.

A remote workspace is one of the most important aspects of remote work. Many remote workers will spend their entire day in the same room that's not set up for their success. This can affect productivity, happiness, and overall work life. By setting up an effective workspace, you can put yourself in a great position to increase your productivity and enjoy your remote work to its fullest potential. A dedicated office is the ideal situation, but often remote work brings travel and it's common to work from different locations. It will be up to you to identify how to create a conducive work environment no matter where you are. This could mean the local coffee shop or even a beach in Thailand. Regardless of location, there are some key principles you should follow when setting up a good remote workspace.

CHAPTER 6

Managing Time and Productivity as a Digital Nomad

It is important to be flexible with your time; one of the main reasons for being a digital nomad is the freedom to be able to do something when you choose, rather than because you have to. Take advantage of being able to work different hours when you choose and make sure you use your time efficiently so that work doesn't drag on longer than it needs to. If something works well for you on one day, don't be scared to change plans and try something different with your time. A change of scenery can be beneficial for work productivity. A lot of people find that they get more work done in the early hours of the morning so they have more spare time for activities in the day. Others find that splitting their work into two sessions rather than one helps them to get more done and still have a lot of free time. Figure out what works best for you and stick to it. In turn, you will have more time for yourself and more time to travel.

Time management is challenging when life itself is structured around having so much free time. If you are used to the standard

8-hour workday, it is easy to get caught in feeling like you have more time than you actually do. Practice by scheduling your time for a week so that you can see just how much you can fit into a day. You will soon realize that you aren't able to do everything you want to in the week. From there, you can start to plan and set goals with tasks for given days.

CHAPTER 7

Balancing Work and Personal Life

At times, you may need to remind yourself of the reasons why you are a digital nomad. Chances are one of these reasons was to see more of the world and have more experiences. With this in mind, you will want to make your personal life a priority. This doesn't mean you have to be doing something adventurous and exotic every day, but even simple things like exercise, cooking local foods, or meeting new people can add a lot to your travel experience.

One approach that can help is to set a schedule of working hours and personal hours. This doesn't have to be a fixed timetable, and you should try to be flexible, but having a guideline of what time of day you will work will make it easier to allocate personal time. It is very important to have time when you are not thinking about work at all. Often changing locations can be an effective way to transition between work and personal time. For example, you might work at a cafe, then go relax at the beach, or go sightseeing after a day of work at a museum.

Balancing work and playtime isn't just about limiting work hours, but also about making the most of the time you allocate to each. Digital nomads often enjoy their work, so it is tempting to keep doing 'just a little more' work. While having the freedom to spend a few more hours on a project is great, long work hours can lead to burnout and a feeling of being constantly tied to work responsibilities. At the same time, if you only put in the minimum hours, you won't be making the most of the freedom that comes with being a digital nomad. It will take a bit of trial and error to find the right balance, and it may vary depending on what projects you are working on.

Balancing your work with your personal life can be difficult no matter where you are working. Digital nomads will often face additional challenges in this area due to the nature of their work. As a digital nomad, you will find yourself working in various locations from your hotel room to internet cafes, and from clients' offices to libraries. This can make it difficult to separate work time from personal time. It is often too easy to work too much when the office is just 10 steps away. At other times, you might find it difficult to motivate yourself to work and will end up wasting time on activities that belong in your personal life.

CHAPTER 8

Overcoming Challenges of Working from Anywhere

Make the most of good weather or days when there is less work and get out and do something interesting. A few hours work in the morning on a good day can be followed by a trip to the beach or a walk in the hills, leaving the rest of the day work-free. If you take the time to examine when and where you are most productive you will find it is often when deadlines are approaching and the environment in which you work can have big impact on productivity. Try and identify the most inspiring times and places to work and make a habit of doing work at these times, so that the rest of time can be more enjoyable and less guilt ridden. This is much easier to do abroad where a new and exciting place can often be more inspiring than sitting in the same room you always work in.

As any significant shift in life choices, adopting the lifestyle of a digital nomad will not come without its challenges. Those seeking an easy transition should be sufficiently aware of what lies ahead in order to better prepare for and grasp on such challenges. This chapter offers a map of what potential areas may pose problem to the digital work on the move. With understanding of what problems and hitches may arise there is a better chance of successfully avoiding or overcoming them. Working abroad, especially in developing countries, is very different to working at home. Understanding these differences can help you find solutions to the problems and ensure that your work runs smoothly. Adapting your working practice can avoid unnecessary discomfort and frustration. Some people would like to maintain the same working pattern as they did at home, but this is the perfect time to break away from a rigid work timetable and start being more flexible.

CHAPTER 9

Maintaining a Healthy Lifestyle as a Digital Nomad

5. Stay moderate with alcohol – something that can be tough for digital nomads! An occasional drink is OK, but alcohol is both high in calories and bad for willpower when it comes to unhealthy snack choices. A mandatory nightcap every night is also a sure way to feel groggy and unmotivated the next day.

4. Avoid fast food and snacking when sightseeing. This is a sure-fire way to ruin all your good healthy living intentions! Pack a bit of trail mix or a piece of fruit in your bag to keep you going, or take a break and have a fresh juice or smoothie. Step off the beaten path and find a small family-owned local café where they will likely make you a fresh sandwich or salad.

3. If the breakfast option is pretty limited, pack some muesli or porridge, powdered milk, a plastic spoon, and a sharp knife. Use the plastic cup provided, or your own Tupperware, and you have a cheap, disposable, and healthy breakfast option.

2. Breakfast is easy and something you can have a lot of control over. Most hotels will have a buffet breakfast and you can easily make a healthy choice here, with fresh whole fruit, eggs, and whole grain toast being available at most places. If possible, take some yogurt and fresh fruit from the supermarket back to your room and keep it in the mini fridge for cereal or snacks throughout the day.

1. Shop for fresh fruit and produce every few days. Find a local supermarket and buy fresh foods in small, manageable amounts to keep them fresh. Stopping daily at local markets is a great way to get out and explore your new surroundings as well. Make sure you wash everything with bottled water and use a fruit and veg wash if traveling in countries with questionable water safety.

All of my tips and advice are for healthy living and clean eating as you travel. I hope this is helpful and remember moderation is key - it's all about balance!

CHAPTER 10

Building a Network and Community

As for an online community, the possibilities are endless. You might start by seeking out blogs by other digital nomads and leaving comments expressing your own views. You could then hunt around for forums or social networking sites where nomads gather and eventually set up your own blog or website to act as a base for your virtual community. Messaging internet friends through Skype or other VOIP services can provide a warmer, more personal interaction while still being cost-effective and easy to fit into your nomadic lifestyle. With these options, you can spend as little or as much time as you like interacting with other travelers and still forge lasting friendships. These can be a comfort on those occasions when you find yourself physically alone.

When you start out as a digital nomad, you might be inclined to keep to yourself and focus solely on your work. This approach will work for a while, especially if you're independent and have a good work ethic. However, you might find yourself feeling disconnected from the world around you and a little lonely. This is the time to find other people in your position and take steps to build a digital nomad community. This can be done quite effectively online and even more effectively in person if you live or travel in areas where other digital nomads are to be found.

CHAPTER 11

Financial Considerations for Digital Nomads

When considering a move to a new city, nomads should research the cost of living to determine if it is feasible on their current income. Factors such as rent, food, transport, and social activities are taken into consideration to give an estimated monthly spend. It's important to overestimate costs and have a financial buffer in case of emergencies, increased living expenses than anticipated, or work dries up for a period of time. Calculating previous monthly spend on various activities can be useful to compare how frugal one is willing to be if trying to save or allocate more money to something such as an investment. This kind of comparison can be done using a budget tracking app such as PocketGuard, which links to bank accounts and categorizes transactions to give an overview of monthly spending.

A flexible lifestyle doesn't necessarily mean a flexible budget. Digital nomads often have the luxury of choosing a city with a low cost of living, but still may find themselves spending more than anticipated. Careful consideration of a budget and regular financial check-ins can help minimize unnecessary spending and maximize saving.

CHAPTER 12

Legal and Visa Requirements for Digital Nomads

Legal and visa issues will always be a contentious subject, as it's a nightmare of paperwork and hassle for some, and others just don't bother. This subject is compounded for a digital nomad who doesn't have a place to call home. Visa runs to neighboring countries can become tedious and expensive just to stay in a country. The days of working under the table are dwindling, and this is not a wise option for ongoing security. Countries such as Estonia have proposed a Digital Nomad Visa to allow location-independent workers to stay in the country for up to a year. This is a step in the right direction and a sign of the changing work landscape. Japan is also considering something similar. At present, however, these visas are few and far between, with most countries not allowing a convenient visa option for digital nomads. The clever and cheap option may be to enroll in a foreign university or take a language course simply to gain access to the country and its amenities and possibly learn something in the process. Education visas can allow various levels of work or none at all, depending on the country, and the headaches and grey areas lie in defining what is study and how much work is allowed. Always read the fine print and be aware that immigration laws are subject to change, so will government interpretation of them. Digital nomads are often at the cutting edge of this, testing the waters to see what they can get away with. An online petition initiated by the digital nomad community is urging countries to adopt standards more suited to remote workers and location-independent entrepreneurs. A failure to do so would see these countries missing out on taxes from a growing demographic and logical contributors to their societies.

CHAPTER 13

Travel Tips and Destinations for Digital Nomads

While there's something to be said about exploring a country or region at a normal pace, and you may still have your opportunity, slow travel is exceptional in that you stay in a foreign land longer than the average holiday maker. You learn the rhythms of daily life and sometimes even pick up a bit of the language. The best way to do this as a digital nomad is to base yourself in a destination where your cost of living will be significantly lower. It's quite possible to live for less in countries like Argentina, Thailand, Turkey, Bulgaria, Hungary, and so on, than it is to have stayed in your home country. Choose places that evoke your creative spirit - places steeped with culture and history, naturally stunning, and socially friendly communities are more likely to enhance your work lifestyle.

Some of the best conversations and epiphanies that I have experienced have been in hostel bars with people that I have known for only a few hours. It's a rite of passage to be huddled with a conglomeration of free spirits, talking about life-changing experiences whilst drinking the drink of that place - be it Turkish Raki, Chilean Pisco, or Thai Whiskey.

As a digital nomad, one casts off the traditional shackles of office life and heads out into the great unknown. It's easy to let their new-found freedom turn into desk-bound isolation. With clients around the world and friends living the conventional...

CHAPTER 14

Digital Nomad Tools and Resources

Digital nomads will benefit from setting themselves up to receive and send faxes abroad as a form of communication and document transfer between businesses, clients, and colleagues. It is fairly cheap and easy to rent a fax number in a foreign country and have the faxes sent directly to an email account. This cuts out the need for a fax machine and gives the digital nomad the freedom to check the incoming faxes from anywhere that they can find internet access. Step now provides a service called fax to email that has local numbers in most countries in the world.

Here we would mention some general digital nomad tools and resources in order for you to create a strong picture in your mind as to all that is available for an entrepreneur abroad. From all of these things to the specific pieces of equipment, i.e. the PDA, Palm Pilot, laptop, cell phone, etc., it is an amazing time in history to be running a business. Task automation and being able to communicate from anywhere in the globe has never been as easy as it is now, and things are only going to continue to progress in this direction. This is good news for digital nomads because it means less time spent doing boring chores and more time being able to separate where we earn our living from what we are truly passionate about in life. All of these tools are part of the mobile office and are likely tax deductible as business expenses.

CHAPTER 15

Success Stories and Inspirations

The last part of the book is spot on, providing aspirational content about people who have been able to achieve the ideal digital nomad lifestyle, detailing how they did it and providing resources for it. A great ending to a great book. This section has reminded me that a lot of people who live the digital nomad way of life are, in fact, entrepreneurs, not necessarily location-independent employees. They are self-contained with their portable lifestyle. In line with this, many entrepreneurs who strive to live the digital nomad lifestyle could learn a lot from already established successful digital nomads, who may have blazed a trail for entrepreneurship in their specific field. You can learn from other successful people and even network to make connections that have the potential to further your own business. This section is almost like a form of career guidance, not just for the nomad, but there are good resources for people who are looking to break away from the typical nine-to-five, location-dependent lifestyle and are seeking a more liberating and fulfilling way of life. This is for anyone wanting to draw inspiration from others in order to make positive changes for themselves in their work and life.

CHAPTER 16

Conclusion

We have reached the final chapter on the Digital Nomads journey. It has been a long trip - we have covered how to get started as a digital nomad, how to manage your finances, how to stay productive, and more. At the beginning of this book, I stated that you can work from anywhere. If you have been following along on your journey, you have already participated in the thought experiments in the first chapter, and now you have gained all the tools necessary for the lifestyle change. The evidence is clear - it's quite clear that with the widespread availability of internet, and a rising trend in output-focused work, the idea of being able to work from anywhere in the world is not only possible, but probable. If it's not available to you now, it will be in the near future. With that being said, the life of a digital nomad is not for everyone, however, it is my belief that if you made it to this final chapter, you should certainly give it a try because at the very least, you have a burning desire to free yourself from the confines of your office and your country. There's no better time to give it a shot than now, and if you don't like it, your old job will surely take you back.

Milton Keynes UK
Ingram Content Group UK Ltd.
UKHW040329031224
452051UK00011B/315